From old photograph found in Savannah.

PORCH OF BULLOCK-HABERSHAM HOUSE, SAVANNAH, GA.

Built about 1818 for Archibald Bullock, by the Architect, William Jay. Torn down 1914.

Lost Examples of Colonial Architecture

Buildings that have disappeared
or been so altered as to be denatured

by

JOHN MEAD HOWELLS

With an Introduction by

FISKE KIMBALL

DOVER PUBLICATIONS, INC.

NEW YORK

Published in Canada by General Publishing Company, Ltd., 30 Lesmill Road, Don Mills, Toronto, Ontario.
Published in the United Kingdom by Constable and Company, Ltd., 10 Orange Street, London WC 2.

This Dover edition, first published in 1963, is an unabridged and unaltered republication of the work originally published by William Helburn, Inc., in 1931, to which has been added a new Index, especially prepared for this Dover edition.

Standard Book Number: 486-21143-6
Library of Congress Catalog Card Number: 63-21679

Manufactured in the United States of America
Dover Publications, Inc.
180 Varick Street
New York, N.Y. 10014

INTRODUCTION

THE idea of this book, so happily conceived by Mr. Howells, is a unique one—to preserve for architects and all lovers of early America the aspect of buildings which have disappeared or which have been so altered as to lose their character and quality. Here is not one building which can be seen today in the form in which it is shown; the volume offers a delightful sedentary tour to monuments of American art which have long vanished, many of them almost unknown to our generation.

The assembling of these views has been no light task nor one likely to be duplicated; some seven years of loving labor has been necessary to track down the buildings shown and the old photographs here brought together for the first time. The work has been made more difficult and the result more valuable by the pains taken to include none but works of real merit in design, adequately recorded by the camera.

To turn these pages is to realize the depth of our artistic and historic loss through the destruction of old buildings by war, by fire, by revolutions of taste, and by the ruthless march of urban "improvement." *Quod non facerunt barbari, fecerunt Barberini*. Thanks to Mr. Howells' pious researches, at least the forms and the flavor of these buildings survive for us.

Much as we deplore the destruction, we must not think its extent peculiar to our own country and time. It has always and everywhere accompanied life and vital growth. Raphael's palaces in the Borgo were swept away after a century to make way for the colonnades of St. Peter. The old quarters of Paris fell before the grandiose *percements* of the Napoleons. We should be more concerned that so little of what has taken the place of our colonial buildings shares their merits of honesty, dignity and beauty.

In other countries there have long existed agencies of the state charged by law with power to forbid or arrest the destruction of buildings of historic or artistic interest. Our constitutions will not permit such a paternal protection of buildings in private ownership .We may console ourselves—if it be a consolation—with the thought that the measures taken elsewhere by government are never entirely efficacious, and rejoice that in this, as in so many matters, private initiative and beneficence have here so often supplied the lack of public action. Individuals, local organizations and the societies in many regions dedicated to the work of preservation have rescued many a fine building and put it beyond further danger.

The duty of recording the artistic heritage surviving or already lost has likewise been assumed, abroad, by the State, in the inventories or surveys of historic monuments published in long series by every European government. Here that task too is left to private endeavor. Fortunate we are that, on one phase of it, Mr. Howells has undertaken the heavy responsibility, and absolved it so admirably as in this volume.

FISKE KIMBALL.

ACKNOWLEDGMENT

VENTURE to offer this word of acknowledgment to those whose unselfish help has made it possible to get together this group of "documents." I have had to trouble many persons with requests not only for photograph material, but for dates and data.

I wish to especially acknowledge the co-operation of the Metropolitan Museum of Art, and its admirably arranged and managed photograph department, as also the Society for the Preservation of New England Antiquities; also the Essex Institute, the New York Historical Society, the Georgia Historical Society, of which Mr. Harden is Librarian; the Museum of Fine Arts, Boston, and its Curator, Mr. Hipkiss; the Historical Societies of Beverly and of Maine; Dartmouth College, Mr. Holland of the Library of Congress, and Mr. Baldwin, Secretary of the American Institute of Architects; Mr. Kocher of the Architectural Record; Mr. Betts, Editor of the American Architect, and Mr. Denmark of the Southern Architect.

Mr. Ogden Codman's permission to use his collections, now in charge of the Metropolitan Museum, and the experience and expert knowledge of Mr. Sumner Appleton, whose cordial co-operation no amount of correspondence has exhausted, have been invaluable, as also the help of Mr. George D. Seymour and Mr. J. Frederick Kelly, both Connecticut experts; of Mr. Andrew Ditmas, the Long Island specialist, and of Mr. Herbert Browne, Mr. W. W. Cordingley, Mr. Albert Hale, Mr. W. H. Kilham, Mr. Robert Bellows, Mr. Charles Stoughton, Mr. Albert Simons, Mr. William Smith, Mr. W. K. Covell, Mr. Wallace Nutting, Mr. Henrik Wallin, Dr. Cornelius Weygandt, Dr. Wallis D. Walker, Mr. Thomas Waterman, Miss Mira Dock and Mr. and Mrs. L. D. Douglas of Pennsylvania, and Miss Alicia Middleton of Rhode Island, besides those whose names I may have omitted.

To Professor Fiske Kimball, Curator of the Pennsylvania Museum of Art, I am especially indebted, not only for the "introduction" to this volume, but for the assistance of his great knowledge of early American architecture.

JOHN MEAD HOWELLS.

LIST OF PLATES
LOST EXAMPLES OF COLONIAL ARCHITECTURE

LIST OF PLATES

LIST OF PLATES

LIST OF PLATES

LIST OF PLATES

LIST OF PLATES

LIST OF PLATES

LIST OF PLATES

LIST OF PLATES

Plate 1

Salem, Washington Square, Salem Common, West Gate

Designed by Samuel McIntire. From a daguerreotype owned by the Essex Institute. Taken before 1850.

PLATE 2

From old plate found in Savannah.

BANK OF UNITED STATES, SAVANNAH BRANCH

*Built 1819. Altered and architecturally denatured 1880. What remained was finally torn down 1924. This photograph shows the original
building as of 1819. The copper plate on the cornerstone named William Jay as the architect with date
(probably of completed building) 1820.*

PLATE 3

McLean Hospital for the Insane, Charlestown (Later Somerville), Mass.

The center building as shown is the Joseph Barrell House, built by Charles Bulfinch, Architect, in 1792. This house and estate purchased by the Asylum in 1818 who engaged Bulfinch to add the wings as shown. NOTE: The projecting wings shown in plate are not at right angles with the back buildings, but slightly more in the courtyard. Bulfinch did this to preserve two rows of fine trees. Built 1792–1818. Taken down about 1898.

PLATE 4

U. S. ASSAY OFFICE, NEW YORK

Built 1822–1824 for the Branch Bank of U. S. Architect, Martin C. Thompson. Occupied as Assay Office 1854, taken down 1915.
(Now in court of Metropolitan Museum of Art.)

PLATE 5

THE ATHENÆUM, PORTSMOUTH, N. H.

*Built 1803. At a later date entire balustrade on the cornice, as well as the left hand curve of the cornice
itself was removed. Also at that or another date, the first building to the right was
denatured by changing the window openings and eliminating the horizontal white
bands. This building originally formed the center of a complete architectural
composition, the left-hand part of which still shows in this plate. The
photograph from which the plate was made is believed to be unique.*

PLATE 6

FIRST LIBRARY BUILDING, PHILADELPHIA, PA.

Built 1789–90. Architect, Dr. William Thornton.

PLATE 7

BANK OF STATE OF GEORGIA, SAVANNAH, GA.

Shown as built for the bank in 1816. Bank of State of Georgia suspended operations as result of the Civil War, building was put to other uses and torn down in 1906.

PLATE 8

BOSTON LIBRARY

*Forming central motif of Franklin Crescent and showing small park and urn in foreground.
Built 1793.*

PLATE 9

FRANKLIN CRESCENT, BOSTON, MASS.

*Known as the Tontine buildings. Laid out by Charles Bulfinch in 1793 after his return from
England, and possibly inspired from a design by the Adam brothers. Bulfinch's plan was a
single crescent with a narrow enclosed park, and the opposite or North side,
straight. The line of the curve may still be seen in the curve of Franklin Street.*

Plate 10

OLD U. S. CUSTOMS HOUSE, CENTRAL STREET, SALEM, MASS.

Doorway, showing eagle carved by Samuel McIntire, in its original position.

PLATE 11

FRANKLIN HALL, THE PARADE, PORTSMOUTH, N. H.

Built 1819. Lafayette held a reception here in 1824. Demolished 1879.

PLATE 12

Courtesy of the Society for the Preservation of New England Antiquities.

BOYLSTON MARKET

Charles Bulfinch, Architect. Built 1809, demolished 1888. Cupola now on Calvary M. E. Church, Arlington, Mass.

PLATE 13

OLD BOSTON CITY HALL

Built 1810. Originally designed and built by Charles Bulfinch as courthouse. Wrecked 1862.

Courtesy of the Bostonian Society.

CUSTOMS HOUSE, BOSTON, MASS.

Before addition of present tower in 1915. Date of building, 1846.
Architect, Ammi Burnham Young.

PLATE 14

OLD EXCHANGE, SAVANNAH, GA.

*The plans were drawn up by Mr. Boucher, and the cornerstone was laid on June 15th, 1799.
Demolished 1904.*

PLATE 15

OLD GUARD HOUSE, SAVANNAH, GA.

Destroyed by earthquake.

PLATE 16

Courtesy of Ernest Ray Denmark, Esq.

THE BRIARS, NATCHEZ, MISS.

Built in 1826 for Capt. William Burr Howell whose daughter, Varina, married Jefferson Davis. Lately restored. Photograph taken before restoration.

Courtesy of Robert Sherlock, Esq.

LIVINGSTON COUNTY COURTHOUSE, GENESEO, N. Y.

Constructed in 1823. Demolished in 1898 to make way for new building.

PLATE 17

TOMBS PRISON, NEW YORK CITY

Plate 18

White House, Washington, D. C.

West front before present additions.

PLATE 19

WAR DEPARTMENT BUILDING, WASHINGTON, D. C.

Showing original condition during Civil War.

PLATE 20

Courtesy of Henrik Wallin, Esq.

CHATHAM COUNTY COURTHOUSE, SAVANNAH, GA.

Built 1833. Taken down 1889.

PLATE 21

OLD DARTMOUTH HALL, DARTMOUTH COLLEGE

Built 1784. Destroyed by fire 1904.

PLATE 22

MERCHANTS EXCHANGE, STATE STREET, BOSTON

Built 1842. Destroyed 1889.

PLATE 23

BRAZER'S BUILDING, STATE STREET, BOSTON

Taken just before demolition. This building shows somewhat the vertical simplicity of some of the most modern European buildings.

PLATE 24

NEW HAMPSHIRE BANK

Built 1802. Lawyers offices above the bank were occupied by President Franklin Pierce. Name of architect, Eliphilet Ladd.

PLATE 25

OLD COLLEGE TAVERN

Photographed in 1899, showing in background Grant's Tomb, which was finished in 1897.

PLATE 26

SIMPSON TAVERN, MEDFORD, MASS.

Built 1756. Destroyed 1915.

Courtesy of Ogden Codman, Esq.

PLATE 27

George E. Noyes Negative.

Poore Tavern (About 1650), Old Newbury

Destroyed about 1900. Tavern sign now preserved in Historical Society.

PLATE 28

Photograph by Wm. H. Tea.   *Courtesy of Mrs. Lingle D. Douglas.*

CATHOLIC ORPHANAGE, READING, PA.
Built about 1770. Destruction date unknown.

Photograph by Wm. H. Tea.   *Courtesy of Mrs. Lingle D. Douglas.*

TRINITY LUTHERAN PAROCHIAL SCHOOL, READING, PA.
Building date unknown. Destroyed about 1892.

Plate 29

Courtesy of Dr. Cornelius Weygandt.

BROTHERS HOUSE OF THE SEVENTH DAY BAPTISTS, EPHRATA, PA.
Built early in Eighteenth Century.

Courtesy of Miss Mira L. Dock.

MANADA FURNACE
Ruins of primitive iron reduction furnace known as Manada Furnace, near Manada Gap, Pa.
Built 1835. Fallen down through decay.

PLATE 30

Bohn Negative.

ERASMUS HALL, FLATBUSH AVENUE NEAR CHURCH AVENUE, BROOKLYN

Built 1786. Soon to be removed.

PLATE 31

INDEPENDENT PRESBYTERIAN CHURCH, SAVANNAH, GA.

Built 1819. Destroyed by fire 1889. John H. Greene, Architect, who also built in 1815 the First Congregational Church in Providence, R. I., which this greatly resembles. The Providence church is reputed to be from a design by Sir Christopher Wren. The church was rebuilt soon after destruction. This plate shows the original building.

PLATE 32

Reproduced from an old photograph in the possession of the Cuyaga County Historical Society.

FIRST PRESBYTERIAN CHURCH, AUBURN, N. Y.

Built in 1816. Torn down 1869.

PLATE 33

NEW SOUTH CHURCH, BOSTON, MASS.

Mr. Bulfinch was commissioned to build this church on the Church Green at Bedford and Summer Streets. This church was octagonal in plan and built of hammered granite and, "seems to have been universally considered the most beautiful of all his churches." Built 1814. Taken down 1868.

PLATE 34

NEW SOUTH CHURCH, BOSTON, MASS.

Doric portico, Charles Bulfinch, Architect. Built 1814. Taken down 1868.

PLATE 35

HOLY CROSS CHURCH, BOSTON, MASS.

Built 1800. Charles Bulfinch, Architect. Foot of Franklin Street just below Franklin Crescent.

PLATE 36

SALEM SOUTH CHURCH

Designed by Samuel McIntire. Destroyed by fire in 1903.

PLATE 37

George E. Noyes Negative.

ST. PAUL'S CHURCH (1800), HIGH STREET HEAD OF MARKET STREET,
NEWBURYPORT, MASS.

Burned down about 1920.

PLATE 38

BELLEVILLE CONGREGATIONAL CHURCH (OLD), HIGH STREET,
NEWBURYPORT, MASS.

Built 1816. Burned 1867.

PLATE 39

OLD CHURCH AT LYME, CONN.

*Designed and built by Col. Samuel Belcher, 1817, showing original building before
its destruction by fire in 1907.*

Plate 40

St. Paul's Church, Augusta, Ga.

From a photograph of the original building before its destruction by fire in 1916. It has since been rebuilt.

PLATE 41

COLLEGIATE REFORMED CHURCH OF HARLEM

PLATE 42

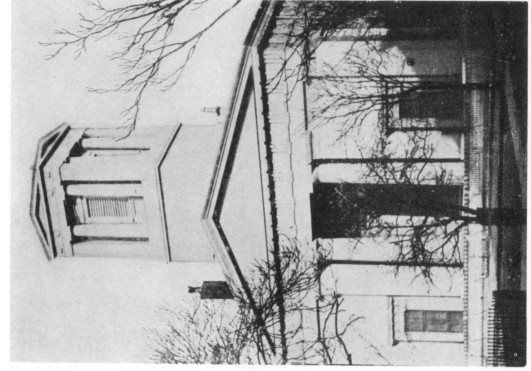

ST. BARTHOLOMEW'S
GREAT JONES STREET AND LAFAYETTE PLACE, N. Y.

COLLEGIATE REFORMED CHURCH
N. W. CORNER LAFAYETTE PLACE AND FOURTH STREET, N. Y.

PLATE 43

SHILOH PRESBYTERIAN CHURCH
SPRING AND MARION STREETS, N. Y.

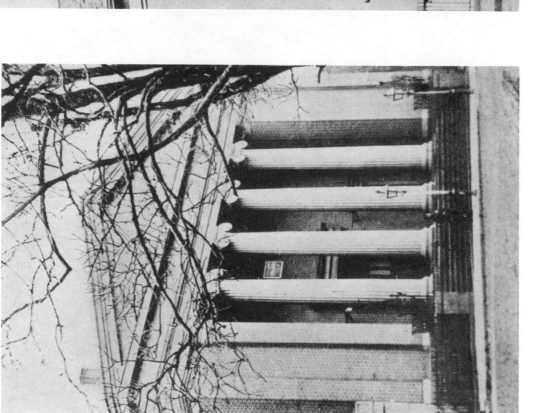

THIRD UNIVERSALIST CHURCH
BLEECKER STREET, N. Y.

PLATE 44

PULPIT IN INDEPENDENT PRESBYTERIAN CHURCH, SAVANNAH, GA.

Photograph taken in original building before destruction by fire in 1889.

PLATE 45

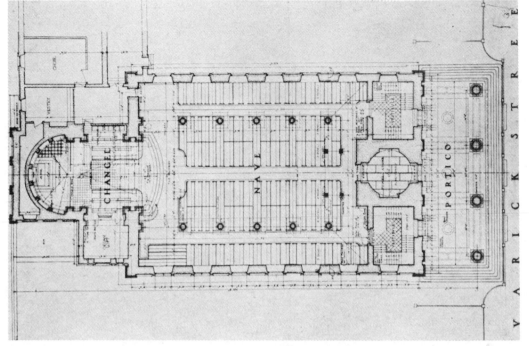

FIRST FLOOR PLAN OF ST. JOHN'S CHAPEL

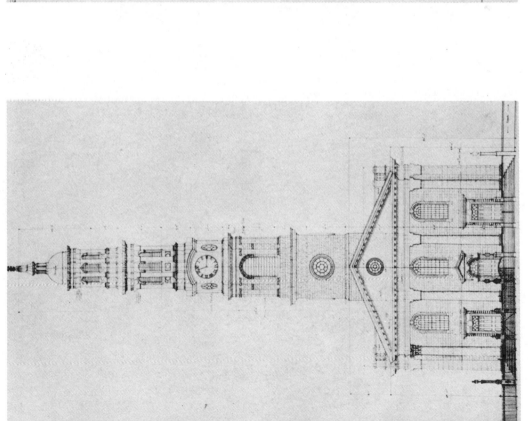

FRONT ELEVATION OF ST. JOHN'S CHAPEL

PLATE 46

Courtesy of Metropolitan Museum of Art.

ST. JOHN'S CHAPEL, NEW YORK

View of apse. Built 1803–7. Architects, John & Isaac McComb. Demolished 1918.

PLATE 47

INTERIOR ST. PAUL'S CHURCH, NEWBURYPORT

PLATE 48

VAN NESS MANSION, WASHINGTON, D. C.
Designed by Benjamin Henry Latrobe 1813. Demolished in 1908. The Pan-American Building occupies its site.

VAN NESS MANSION, WASHINGTON, D. C.
Designed by Benjamin Henry Latrobe 1813. Demolished in 1908. The Pan-American Building occupies its site.

PLATE 49

From the Ogden Codman Collection.

UNIDENTIFIED TOWN HOUSE

PLATE 50

BURD HOUSE, PHILADELPHIA, PA.

Benjamin Henry Latrobe, Architect. Built 1800. Removal date not known.

PLATE 51

STREET ALONG CANAL ABOVE PRESENT KEY BRIDGE, GEORGETOWN, D. C.

COMMODORE JOHN RODGERS HOUSE, WASHINGTON, D. C

Built 1820. Later occupied by James G. Blaine. Site now covered by Belasco Theatre.

PLATE 52

CORNER HOUSE IN PHILADELPHIA, PA.

Now removed or altered into shops.

Plate 53

Houses Formerly Standing on East Side of Middle Street, Lancaster, Pa.
Showing Early Half-Timber Construction

PLATE 54

BULLOCK-HABERSHAM HOUSE, SAVANNAH, GA.

Built about 1818 for Archibald Bullock, by the Architect, William Jay. Torn down 1914.

HUBER OR ELLIOTT HOUSE, SAVANNAH, GA.

Now destroyed. Stood on corner of Oglethorpe Square.

Plate 55

Scarborouge House, Savannah, Ga.
Detail of south porch, showing original iron work.

Plate 56

Missroon House, Charleston, S. C.

Built on the site of Granvilles Bastion, the colonial fortification, whose walls form part of the foundation of the dwelling. This building was damaged in the storm of 1911 and left unoccupied until 1925. The photograph shows it at that time. It has since been enlarged and altered exteriorally, but the interior was carefully restored.

PLATE 57

HOLMES HOUSE, CHARLESTON, S. C.

One of the first homes built on East Bay in the Battery. The structure is built entirely of plantation-made materials and erected by plantation labor. It stood on the site of Fort Mechanic, which had been built in 1798 as a preparation against expected hostilities with France. Built 1820. Demolished circa 1913.

PLATE 58

MANSION HOUSE, BROAD STREET, CHARLESTON, S. C.

Built circa 1765. Destroyed 1927.

PLATE 59

Courtesy of Andrew Ditmas, Esq.

CORTELYOU HOUSE, SOUTH BROOKLYN

1699. This date inlaid in Dutch lead in gable, not shown in plate. Today a roofless ruin buried nearly to the eaves.

Plate 60

Houses Formerly at 69–71 Charlton Street, New York

Built first quarter of nineteenth century. Lately destroyed.

PLATE 61

LA GRANGE TERRACE, LATER CALLED COLONNADE ROW

Consisting originally of nine separate residences on Lafayette Place, of which four are still standing (1917); was erected in 1831. They were designed by Mr. (Seth) Geer, and all stone work was executed by state prisoners at Sing Sing. One-half of row pulled down about 1900. La Grange Terrace was so named after Lafayette's country seat in France.

PLATE 62

COLONNADE ROW (LA GRANGE TERRACE), N. Y.

Facade of a single unit.

PLATE 63

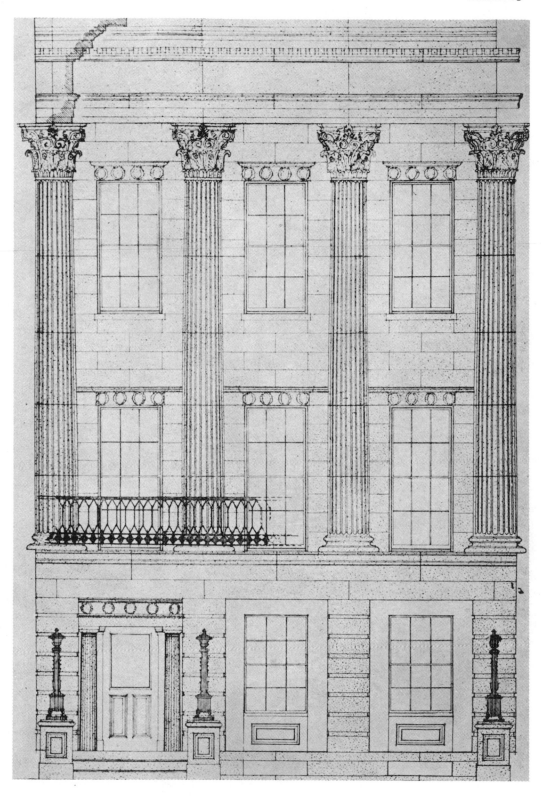

COLONNADE ROW (LA GRANGE TERRACE), N. Y.

Measured drawing of the facade of a single unit.

Plate 64

Photographed for Charles F. McKim, Esq.

Sueton Grant, or Atkinson House, Thames Street, Newport, R. I.

Circa 1675. Destroyed many years ago.

PLATE 65

HOME OF WILLIAM ELLERY, NEWPORT, R. I.

Upper Thames Street, near Poplar and Farewell Streets. Torn down about twenty-five years ago.

PLATE 66

NATHAN SMITH HOUSE, ELM STREET, NEW HAVEN, CONN.

1816. David Hoadley, Architect. Demolished to provide site for the present New Haven County Courthouse, 1910–11. Wrought iron railings and urns now incorporated in the New Haven Colonial Historical Society's new building.

PLATE 67

DOORWAY, NATHAN SMITH HOUSE, ELM STREET, NEW HAVEN, CONN. (1816)

PLATE 68

MATTHEW COBB HOUSE, PORTLAND, MAINE

Built 1801. Taken down 1895.

PLATE 69

HANCOCK HOUSE, BEACON STREET, BOSTON

Built 1737 by Thomas Hancock, uncle of John Hancock, whom he adopted.
Demolished in 1863.

PLATE 70

AMORY-TICKNOR HOUSE, BOSTON

Built about 1803. Showing architect's original design before alteration into two dwellings. Altered later.

HINCKLEY HOUSE (ON CORNER), BOSTON

Purchased by the Somerset Club in 1852.

PLATE 71

AMORY-TICKNOR HOUSE, BOSTON

*Probably by Bulfinch, who designed the adjoining houses. Amory, on completion, invited friends
to a house warming, but learned of his own bankruptcy before the arrival of his guests.
Built about 1803. Altered to two dwellings at later date. Now altered to shop fronts.*

PLATE 72

COLONNADE ROW, BOSTON

Built 1810. South corner of West and Tremont Streets. Charles Bulfinch, Architect.

PLATE 73

THREE HOUSES, CORNER AT BEACON AND JOY STREETS, BOSTON

The two nearest houses are standing, though somewhat altered. The third house is gone.

PLATE 74

WILLIAM PERKINS HOUSE, GARDEN VIEW

*Formerly at corner of Mt. Vernon and Joy Streets. William Perkins lived here from 1861 to 1883.
Building date unknown.*

PLATE 75

WILLIAM PERKINS HOUSE

Formerly at corner of Mt. Vernon and Joy Streets. William Perkins lived here from 1861 to 1883.
Building date unknown.

PLATE 76

Courtesy of the Metropolitan Museum of Art.

WELLES-GRAY HOUSES, SUMMER STREET, BOSTON

PLATE 77

WELLES-GRAY HOUSES, SUMMER STREET CORNER OF KINGSTON STREET,
BOSTON, MASS.

PLATE 78

HOUSES OF EDWARD EVERETT AND DANIEL DENNY
Formerly at Summer and Otis Streets, Boston.

PLATE 79

HOME OF THOMAS WIGGLEWORTH
FRANKLIN PLACE, NORTH SIDE, ACROSS FROM CRESCENT

Built 1795. Charles Bulfinch, Architect. Taken down 1858.

PLATE 80

Courtesy of the Society for the Preservation of New England Antiquities.

TWIN HOUSES OF GRANITE, FORMERLY IN WINTHROP PLACE, BOSTON

PLATE 81

TUFTS HOUSE, DORCHESTER, MASS.

Formerly at Northeast corner of Chelsea and Prospect Streets.

PLATE 82

TREMERE HOUSE, NORTH STREET, BOSTON

Built 1680. Line of original gable is easily discernible in brick work where the third story has been added.

PLATE 83

HOUSE FORMERLY ON ALDEN STREET OFF SUDBURY STREET, BOSTON

Built in 1762 by James Gardner. In 1788 it was described as "that elegant brick dwelling house," and was sold to William Wetmore for Five hundred and thirty pounds Sterling.

PLATE 84

PARKMAN HOUSES, BOWDOIN SQUARE, BOSTON

Built about 1808. Demolition date unknown. Two houses built as one block by Samuel Parkman for his two married daughters. A design for these houses one story less in height is preserved among the Bulfinch drawings of the Massachusetts Institute of Technology. The garlands in panels under the windows resemble the same motif on the Bulfinch House, Bulfinch Place.

Plate 85

JAMES SWAN HOUSE, DORCHESTER, MASS.

Ascribed to Bulfinch. A balustrade, as shown on wings, originally also encircled top. Circa 1796. Destruction date unknown.

Plate 86

NILES-GARDNER HOUSE, DORCHESTER, MASS.

Pre-Revolutionary. Round ends added somewhat later. One of the interiors was papered with news journals giving important events of those times. Demolished 1890.

PLATE 87

THWING-BARTLETT HOUSE, WASHINGTON AND BARTLETT STREETS, ROXBURY, MASS.

This was a double house (with porch column on center line) occupied by the Thwing and Bartlett families. Built about 1825. Demolished 1900.

Plate 88

39 AND 40 BEACON STREET, BOSTON, MASS.

*Built 1818. No. 39 shows the original appearance of the Nathan Appleton House now completely
altered. No. 40 is the Parker-Inches House, to which a store has also been added.*

TWIN HOUSES AT 47–48 BEACON STREET, BOSTON, MASS.

Showing original condition.

PLATE 89

Courtesy of the Essex Institute.

LEWIS HUNT HOUSE, WASHINGTON STREET CORNER LYNDE STREET, SALEM

1698. Taken down 1863. Now (1926) Odell Block.

PLATE 90

EZEKIEL HERSEY DERBY HOUSE, 204–6 ESSEX STREET, SALEM

1799 by Bulfinch, later residence of Benjamin W. Crowninshield and Richard Rogers, 1817.
Bought by William Maynes, 1874, and altered to Maynes Block in 1908.

Courtesy of the Essex Institute.

PLATE 91

TIMOTHY ORNE HOUSE, 266 ESSEX STREET, SALEM, MASS.
1761. Later residence of Benjamin Hodges. Taken down before 1913.

PLATE 92

DUDLEY WOODBRIDGE HOUSE, 48 BRIDGE STREET, SALEM

Built about 1786. Interiors partially removed 1930. McIntire's original plan exists for this house, showing it to be his authentic work.
Plate shows condition of house as photographed by Cousins about 1900.

PLATE 93

GIDEON TUCKER HOUSE (1800), 129 ESSEX STREET, SALEM

Samuel McIntire, Architect. Now (1926) Father Mathew Society. Porch removed to Essex Institute.

PLATE 94

CAPTAIN JOSEPH PEABODY HOUSE, 136 ESSEX STREET, SALEM

*Built 1820 for son, Joseph Augustus Peabody. Partly on site of Emmanuel Downing House.
Used as State Armory, 1890–1908. New armory built 1908.*

PLATE 95

JOSEPH J. KNAPP HOUSE, 85 ESSEX STREET, SALEM, MASS.

Built before 1802. Removed to Curtis Street in 1895. Plate shows house in original position.

Courtesy of the Essex Institute.

MRS. MARY ANN SANDERS HOUSE, ESSEX STREET, SALEM, MASS.

Alexander Graham Bell here developed the telephone, 1873–76.
Y. M. C. A. building now on site.

PLATE 96

SIMON FORRESTER HOUSE, 188 DERBY STREET, SALEM

Built 1790–91. No longer standing.

HUBON HOUSE, 48 CHARTER STREET, SALEM

1780—removed 1906.

PLATE 97

Courtesy of the Essex Institute.

AARON WAITE HOUSE, 376 ESSEX STREET, SALEM

Built 1789–90. Later residence of Nathaniel L. Rogers. Taken down 1902.

DOORWAY OF AARON WAITE HOUSE, 376 ESSEX STREET, SALEM

Later owned by Nathaniel L. Rogers. Built 1789–90. Taken down 1902.

PLATE 98

JOSEPH FELT HOUSE (1809), 153 LAFAYETTE STREET, SALEM

*Designed by Samuel McIntire. Later Capt. Roundy House, and occupied by
William O. Chapman at time it was burned, June 25th, 1924.*

WEST HOUSE, 194 LAFAYETTE STREET, SALEM

Built 1844. Destroyed by fire 1914.

PLATE 99

JOSIAH DOW HOUSE (1787), LAFAYETTE STREET, SALEM

By Samuel McIntire, later Osgood House, Mayor John G. Hurley, 1900, French Catholic Rectory, 1908, taken down 1909.

134 ESSEX STREET, SALEM, MASS.

This site was once occupied by Emmanuel Downing, whose son removed to London, and gave his name to Downing Street.

PLATE 100

Courtesy of Miss Henrietta Kilham.

CABOT-LEE-KILHAM HOUSE, 115 CABOT STREET, BEVERLY, MASS.

Built 1773. Lately destroyed to make way for a gasoline station.

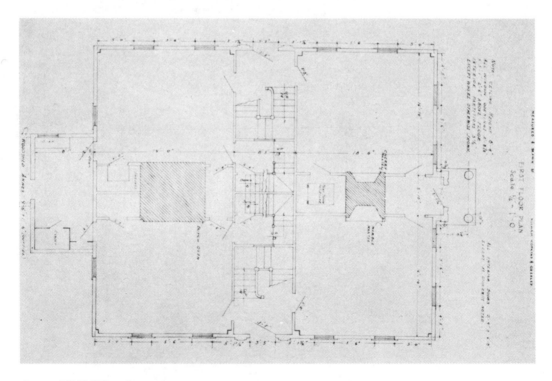

Courtesy of W. H. Kilham, Esq.

CABOT-LEE-KILHAM HOUSE, 115 CABOT STREET, BEVERLY, MASS.

Ground floor plan. Built 1773. Lately destroyed to make way for a gasoline station.

PLATE 101

Courtesy of Mrs. Stephen Decatur.

ADMIRAL STORER HOUSE, PORTSMOUTH, N. H.

*By some claimed to be by Bulfinch. Destroyed about 1880 to give place to the Frank Jones
Mansion. (Compare with the Octagon of Washington, D. C., by Dr. Thornton.
Both Thornton and Bulfinch worked on the Capitol.)*

PLATE 102

Courtesy of Alfred Gooding, Esq.

HAVEN HOUSE, PORTSMOUTH, N. H.

On site of present high school.

WOODBURY-LANGDON HOUSE

Woodwork from octagon room in the Woodbury-Langdon House. Built 1785.
Shown as now set up in the new Rockingham Hotel about 1880.

PLATE 103

BOYD-RAYNER HOUSE, PORTSMOUTH, N. H.

*Built circa 1740. In 1768 Col. Boyd "considerably enlarged it." (We can guess that this
addition is the part that shows in the photograph beyond the third chimney since,
without this, the house is complete and symmetrical with its "whale-walk"
and doorway properly centered.)*

JUDGE SHERBURNE HOUSE

*Built circa 1760. Demolished 1924. Judge Sherburne's son John was an officer
in the Revolution.*

PLATE 104

GEORGE JAFFREY HOUSE, PORTSMOUTH, N. H.

Side and rear view. Built about 1730. Demolished 1920.

GEORGE JAFFREY HOUSE, PORTSMOUTH, N. H.

View of entrance front just prior to demolition. Built about 1730. Demolished 1920.

PLATE 105

JOHN CHIPMAN HOUSE, 422 ESSEX STREET, SALEM

Burned 1914. Date of construction unknown.

29–35 TONTINE BLOCK, WARREN STREET, SALEM, MASS.

Burned 1914.

Plate 106

Hill House, Portsmouth, N. H.

Formerly at Vaughn and Hanover Streets. Construction date not known, but deeded in 1750 by Brewster to his son. In 1777 Capt. David Cullum brought his bride to this house to start housekeeping. He had fought as a lieutenant under Paul Jones in either the "Ranger," or the "Bonhomme Richard."

PLATE 107

FRONT DOOR OF TAYLOR HOUSE, THAMES STREET, NEWPORT, R. I.

Built 1750. Door itself now removed to Historical Society's headquarters.
Photograph presented by Charles F. McKim to W. D. Howells in 1875.

PLATE 108

19 Margin Street, Salem, Mass.

Doorway of house formerly on site of Asiatic Building, 125 Washington Street, removed at building of tunnel, 1838. Destroyed by fire 1914. Moved from 125 Washington Street, name of original house unknown.

PLATE 109

DUDLEY WOODBRIDGE HOUSE, 48 BRIDGE STREET, SALEM

Side door. Built about 1786.

PLATE 110

PINEAPPLE DOORWAY, CAPTAIN THOMAS PAYNTON HOUSE,
BROWN STREET, COURT 7, SALEM, MASS.

In original position. Now removed to Essex Institute.

PLATE 111

6 DOWNING STREET HOUSE, SALEM
Built 1750. Burned 1914.

PLATE 112

Courtesy of the Essex Institute.

JOSEPH J. KNAPP HOUSE, 85 ESSEX STREET, SALEM, MASS.

Doorway, before 1802. Removed to Curtis Street, 1895.

PLATE 113

DOORWAY, BENJAMIN PICKMAN HOUSE (1743), 165 ESSEX STREET, SALEM
Standing today as shown, but built out by buildings in front.

PLATE 114

Courtesy of William Sumner Appleton, Esq.

DOORWAY

*In its original position in village square, Brookline, Mass.
Now removed and placed on the house of Dr. Clifford.*

PLATE 115

ENTRANCE DOOR TO THE J. HEAD HOUSE

Formerly at corner of Tremont and Boylston Streets, Boston.

PLATE 116

George E. Noyes Negative.

DOOR, 71 STATE STREET, NEWBURYPORT, MASS.

*Destroyed about 1924 and altered to store. Bought by the Society for the
Preservation of New England Antiquities.*

PLATE 117

George E. Noyes Negative.

DOOR, 75 STATE STREET, NEWBURYPORT, MASS.

Destroyed. Altered to store about 1918.

Plate 118

George E. Noyes Negative.

Door Posts, Islington Street, Portsmouth, N. H.
Now shops built in front.

PLATE 119

OLD NEW YORK DOORWAY

PLATE 120

NEW YORK HOUSE, FORMERLY AT 85 SOUTH 5TH AVENUE

PLATE 121

DOOR OF HOUSE FORMERLY AT 51 VAN DAM STREET, NEW YORK CITY

PLATE 122

NEW YORK HOUSE, FORMERLY AT 51 CHARLTON STREET

PLATE 123

Courtesy of Ogden Codman, Esq.

DOORWAY OF A NEW YORK HOUSE

Courtesy of Ogden Codman, Esq.

FRONT DOOR OF A NEW YORK HOUSE

PLATE 124

AMASA DAVIS HOUSE, 1234 WASHINGTON STREET, BOSTON

PLATE 125

"CONCORD"

The residence of the first Spanish governor, on the river near Natchez, Miss. Probably built shortly after Revolutionary War. Burned in 1902.

PLATE 126

MONTICELLO, NATCHEZ, MISS.

The home of Major Schotaol, an English officer in the employ of the Spanish governor.
Built probably shortly after the Revolutionary War. Burned in 1901.

PLATE 127

Photograph by Cook, Richmond, Va.

TEDINGTON, JAMES RIVER, VA.

Built 1777. Destroyed by fire 1928.

THE HERMITAGE, OUTSIDE OF SAVANNAH, GA.

Detail of porch.

PLATE 129

THE HERMITAGE, OUTSIDE OF SAVANNAH, GA.

Designed and built by its owner, Henry McAlpin, about 1830. Bulk of house still standing much dilapidated since this photograph.

Courtesy of Andrew Ditmas, Esq.

LEFFERTS HOUSE

Formerly at 563 Flatbush Avenue, Brooklyn. Built during Revolution. Presumably duplicate of an earlier house. Porch and some Hepplewhite motifs added in 1835. Moved to Prospect Park 1918.

PLATE 130

Photograph by Cook, Richmond, Va.

EDGE HILL, VIRGINIA
Home of daughter of Thomas Jefferson. Destroyed by fire 1925.

Courtesy of A. Lawrence Kocher, Esq.

WILLIAMSBURG ROAD, RICHMOND, VA.
*Typical before 1700. Showing log cabin construction under
clapboards and primitive mud chimney.*

PLATE 131

Photograph by Cook, Richmond, Va.

MONTPELIER, ORANGE CO., VA.
*Home of President Madison. Plate shows building before present
alterations and raising of wings.*

Photograph by Cook, Richmond, Va.

DUNGENESS, JAMES RIVER, VA.
Destroyed by fire.

PLATE 132

Photograph by Cook, Richmond, Va.

AMPHILL, CARY HOUSE, CHESTERFIELD CO., VA.

Taken down and reconstructed on Cary Street Road.

Photograph by Cook, Richmond, Va.

RED HILL, CHARLOTTE CO., VA.

Home of Patrick Henry. Burned in 1920.

PLATE 133

Photograph by Cook, Richmond, Va.

ROSEWELL, GLOUCESTER CO., VA.

Burned about 1915. Walls still standing.

Photograph by Cook, Richmond, Va.

CHESTERFIELD COUNTY COURTHOUSE

Built 1752. Pulled down 1911.

PLATE 134

CLEVE MANOR, IN THE RAPPAHANNOCK VALLEY, VIRGINIA
Building date uncertain. Given variously from 1728 to 1754. Destroyed by fire about 1918.

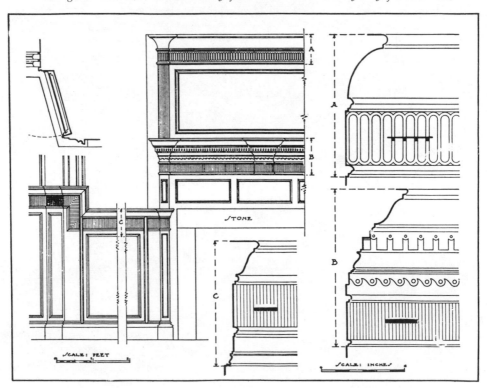

CLEVE MANOR, IN THE RAPPAHANNOCK VALLEY, VIRGINIA
Detail of mantel and window reveal in dining room.

PLATE 135

FENWICK, BRITISH HEADQUARTERS ON JOHNS ISLAND, NEAR CHARLESTON, S. C.

*Built by the Hon. Edward Fenwick, circa 1750. Octagonal wing added probably circa 1790.
Photograph taken before building was purchased and restored by present owner.*

PLATE 136

DOWER HOUSE, NEAR MARLBORO, R. O., PRINCE GEORGE COUNTY, MD.

PLATE 137

SABINE HALL, RICHMOND COUNTY, VA.

Circa 1730. This plate shows the house before present alterations and additions.

PLATE 138

FAIRFIELD, CARTER'S CREEK, GLOUCESTER COUNTY, VA.

Destroyed by fire in early 90's.

Photograph by Cook, Richmond, Va.

PLATE 139

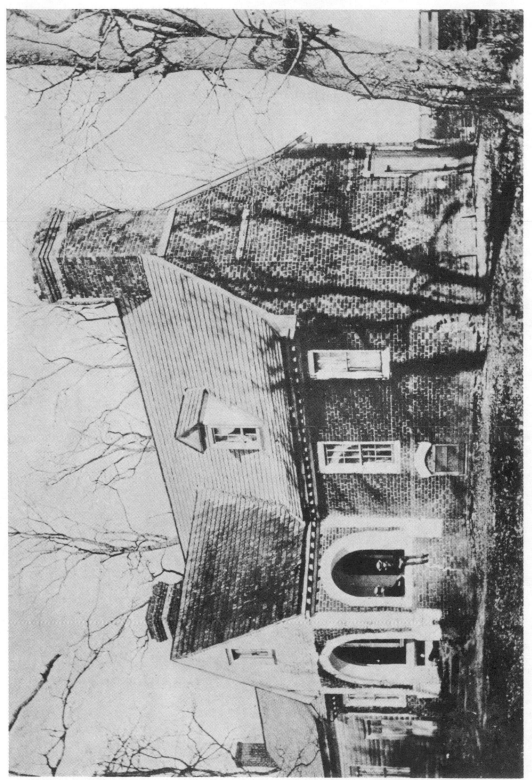

Photograph by Cook, Richmond, Va.

MALBERN HALL, CHARLES CITY COUNTY, VA.

Burned about 1915.

PLATE 140

From a Brady Negative taken 1868.   *Courtesy of Leicester Holland, Esq.*

THE BURNES COTTAGE, WASHINGTON, D. C.

On site now occupied by Pan-American Building.

Courtesy of Dr. Cornelius Weygandt.

DUTCH COLONIAL BARN, EAGLEPOINT, PA.

Legend on cut.

PLATE 141

Courtesy of G. H. Edgell, Dean of Harvard Architectural School.

TRUE DUTCH GABLE, PROBABLY BEFORE 1700, ALBANY

Brick work same as in Amsterdam.

Plate 142

HEGEMAN HOUSE, KINGS HIGHWAY AND FLATBUSH AVENUE, BROOKLYN

Revolutionary. Demolished about 1910.

PLATE 143

DOORWAY, FLATLANDS, BROOKLYN
Now destroyed.

PLATE 144

Bohn Negative.

DOORWAY OF GARRET KOUWENHOVEN HOUSE
KINGS HIGHWAY AND UTICA AVENUE

Pre-Revolutionary. Destroyed 1922.

PLATE 145

DOORWAY OF HOUSE ON KINGS HIGHWAY, FLATLANDS
Built 1812.

PLATE 146

THE GRANGE

*Built 1802 by Alexander Hamilton. Occupied by him as his country seat up to his death in 1814.
Now removed from its original position at 143rd Street and Old Kingsbridge Road to
141st Street and Convent Avenue and occupied as St. Luke's Rectory. This plate
shows the building in its original position. Architect, John McComb.*

HUNT MANSION, HUNTS POINT, N. Y.

Built 1688. This photograph taken about 1886.

PLATE 147

Nash Negative. Courtesy of the Metropolitan Museum of Art.

HAVEMEYER-STRONG HOUSE, THROGGS NECK, N. Y.

Built in the first half of the Nineteenth Century.

Courtesy of Charles W. Stoughton, Esq.

GOUVERNEUR MORRIS MANSION, "OLD MORRISANIA," N. Y.

Built 1789, disappeared about 1900. Mr. Stoughton gives me the note that Mr. Mott (of the Mott Iron Works) bought land adjoining from Mr. Morris and asked if Mr. Morris had any objections to his giving it the name of Mott Haven.)

PLATE 148

Courtesy of Charles W. Stoughton, Esq.

ENTRANCE TO WILLIAM J. MORRIS HOUSE, MORRISANIA, N. Y.

Built 1816. Destroyed about 1924.

PLATE 149

WILLIAM J. MORRIS HOUSE, MORRISANIA, N. Y.

Built 1816. Destroyed about 1924.

PLATE 150

ROCK HALL, FAR ROCKAWAY, L. I.

PLATE 151

HALL MANSION, NEW YORK

*Built circa 1825. Site would now be approximately at the corner of Fifth Avenue and 130th Street. Hall was a prosperous merchant.
This photograph taken 188c, and house was destroyed soon after that.*

PLATE 152

APTHORPE MANSION, NINTH AVENUE AND 91ST STREET, NEW YORK

Served as American and British headquarters in 1776. Built in 1767. Destroyed in 1890.

PLATE 153

TREASON HOUSE, WEST HAVERSTRAW, N. Y.

Building date unknown. Pulled down 1926.

Plate 154

Brenton-Coe House, Thames Street, Newport, R. I.

Built 1720. Fallen into decay, and interior woodwork removed 1921. Photographed for Charles F. McKim, 1875.

PLATE 155

EARLY BRICK CHIMNEY
Unidentified.

Plate 156

Courtesy of Dr. Colman W. Cutler.

Gov. Samuel Huntington House, Norwich Town, Conn.

Circa 1784. Exterior altered in 1871 and again in 1916.

PLATE 157

POINT PLEASANT, OR HERRESHOFF HOUSE, BRISTOL, R. I.

Built 1680, the year of the founding of Bristol.

PLATE 158

MARK ANTHONY DE WOLF HOUSE, BRISTOL, R. I.

Built 1835. Lived in by Mrs. De Wolf Mudge at the time that it was burned, about 1920.

PLATE 159

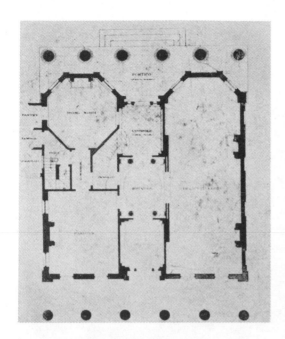
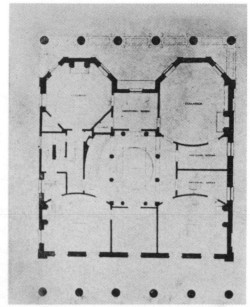

Courtesy of Wallis E. Howe, Esq.

MARK ANTHONY DE WOLF HOUSE, BRISTOL, R. I.

Courtesy of Miss Alicia H. Middleton.

"THE MOUNT," BRISTOL, R. I.

Sunken arch in drawing room, showing original wallpaper. Built 1808 by James De Wolf.
Burned circa 1905.

PLATE 160

Courtesy of Ogden Codman, Esq.

JOSEPH BARRELL HOUSE, CHARLESTOWN (LATER SOMERVILLE), MASS.

*Built 1792. Taken down 1898 and rebuilt in Wayland, Mass., with some modifications.
This plate shows the two center columns of a four column and pediment porch.*

PLATE 161

Courtesy of the Society for the Preservation of New England Antiquities.

EDWARD EVERETT HOUSE, FIVE CORNERS, DORCHESTER, MASS.

PLATE 162

From a photograph by Soule Photo Co.

PEREZ MORTON HOUSE, ROXBURY, MASS.

*This house has a fine floor plan and is undoubtedly by Bulfinch, as Mrs. Morton was Bulfinch's first cousin.
Built 1796. Demolished in the middle 80's.*

PLATE 163

PEREZ MORTON HOUSE, ROXBURY, MASS.

Showing formal layout of stables and out-buildings. The connection to the left of this plate can be seen at the right side of Plate 162.

PLATE 164

PEREZ MORTON HOUSE, ROXBURY, MASS.
Another view.

Plate 165

Shirley Place, Roxbury, Mass.

Showing house in original position with original foundations and with piazzas. Architect, Peter Harrison, according to the best authority.
Built 1746.

Plate 166

SHIRLEY PLACE, ROXBURY, MASS.

*Built 1746. Palladian window as it appeared about the time the Shirley-Eustis House
Association came into possession of the building.*

PLATE 167

SHIRLEY PLACE, ROXBURY, MASS.

East facade as originally completed. Drawings made by and reproduced by courtesy of W. W. Cordingley.

SHIRLEY PLACE, ROXBURY, MASS.

West facade as originally completed.

Courtesy of Ogden Codman, Esq.

SHIRLEY PLACE, ROXBURY, MASS.

Showing dormer and cornice detail, both of which, however, are supposed to be later than original construction.

Plate 168

SUMMER HOUSE AT THE DERBY-OSBORN FARM, PEABODY, MASS.

Erected in 1793 for Elias Hasket Derby, after designs by Samuel McIntire, and removed in 1901 to the estate of William C. Endicott, in Danvers. This plate shows building in original position.

PLATE 169

From a photograph by French.

SUMMER HOUSE AT USHER-ROYALL PLACE, MEDFORD, MASS.

PLATE 170

COGGSWELL HOUSE, ESSEX, MASS.

Built 1739. This house fell down slowly through neglect and was completely demolished by 1924.

JONATHAN WADE GARRISON HOUSE, MEDFORD, MASS.

Built circa 1689. Shown before addition of porch, etc., on entrance side.

PLATE 171

ORIGINAL WENTWORTH HOUSE, CALLED OLD GARRISON HOUSE,
NEAR DOVER, N. H.
Showing condition before present rehabilitation. Built 1685.

GOVERNOR CRADDOCK HOUSE, MEDFORD, MASS.
*Built 1639 by order of Matthew Craddock, first Governor of Massachusetts Company. "It was
built as a fort with windows smaller than shown. A small pane of glass set in iron in
the back wall of the western chimney overlooked the approach from the town."—
from "Our Colonial Homes" by Samuel Adams Drake.*

PLATE 172

Courtesy of the Society for the Preservation of New England Antiquities.

CHAPIN TAVERN (EAST FRONT), CHICOPEE, MASS.

PLATE 173

CHAPIN TAVERN (OVER DOOR, EAST FRONT), CHICOPEE, MASS.

Plate 174

McIntire-Garrison House, York, Maine

Built 1640–1645. Photograph shows house before present restorations.

PLATE 175

HOUSE AT HATFIELD, MASS.

*Building date unknown. Front door motif as shown now in Boston Art Museum. Similar carved work inside destroyed by owner.
Body of house still standing, used as storage barn. Modern house built in front.*

Plate 176

Unidentified Connecticut House of an Early Type

From a very old photograph.

PLATE 177

WHIPPLE HOUSE, IPSWICH, MASS.

Built 1650. Photograph shows house before the present restorations.

PLATE 178

LADY PEPPERELL HOUSE, KITTERY POINT, MAINE

Built 1760. Built apparently as a dower house for Lady Pepperell when Sir William Pepperell's house was to go to their adopted son, who, however, died. Plate shows original condition before addition of side porches in 1922.

Plate 179

Doak House, Marblehead, Mass.

Mentioned by Frank Chouteau Brown in the White Pine Series in Vol. 1, No. 2—1915 as, "a very ancient house indeed which unfortunately has disappeared." Built 1675. Demolished about 1908.

PLATE 180

ROWELL HOUSE, YORKTOWN, VA.

Date unknown. Roofless in 1914, now completely disappeared.

Plate 181

Powell House, Lancaster, Pa.

Showing original half timber construction in gable.

Courtesy of A. Lawrence Kocher, Esq.

PLATE 182

MOULTHROP HOUSE, NEW HAVEN, CONN.

Probably built between 1675 and 1700—taken down 1919. It is thought possible that the original roof on this house was of thatch, owing to the peculiarities of the roof construction.

PLATE 183

HEWLETT HOUSE, WOODBURY, L. I.

Built 1745 by John Hewlett. Taken down 1916.

PLATE 184

ELBERT HOUSE, BROOKLYN
Circa 1667. Now destroyed.

Plate 185

Brinckerhoff House (Now Stagg), Polifly Road (Now Terrace Avenue),
Hasbrouck Heights, Hackensack, N. J.

Plate shows house before present alterations. Roof now changed and "L" destroyed.

PLATE 186

ALBERT LOTT HOUSE, FLATLANDS, BROOKLYN

Circa 1800. Demolished circa 1920.

PLATE 187

BERGEN HOMESTEAD, FLATBUSH, BROOKLYN

Circa 1690. Wings added at later dates. Torn down 1930.

PLATE 188

VAN BRUNT HOUSE, NEW UTRECHT

Built probably shortly after the fire of 1679. Torn down in 1928.

PLATE 189

VAN NIYSE HOUSE, BROOKLYN

Built 1800. Repaired and center dormer added as shown in plate. Since then removed to another site and altered.

Plate 190

Valentine House, Briggs Avenue, New York

Photographed about 1900.

Plate 191

Pump on Vanderveer Farm

Circa 1850.

Van Pelt Well, New Utrecht, Brooklyn

PLATE 192

Courtesy of the Society for the Preservation of New England Antiquities.

NORTON HOUSE, GUILFORD, CONN.

This tiny house was considered by both Mr. Isham and Mr. Kelly as the best remaining example of this very early type. The stone chimney was laid up in clay mortar. It was destroyed by a Polish immigrant who bought the farm. Built 1690. Destroyed 1921.

PLATE 193

Bohn Negative.

REMSEN RYERSON HOUSE, LONG ISLAND
Pre-Revolutionary. Destroyed in 1928.

VANDERBILT HOUSE, FLATBUSH, BROOKLYN

*This was regarded as an Old House during the Revolution. Central dormer as
shown added in 1900. Demolition circa 1925.*

Plate 194

CORNELL-VAN SICLEN HOUSE, NEW LOTS ROAD, BROOKLYN

Pre-Revolutionary. Lately torn down.

MILLWHEEL ON VANDERVEER FARM

Vanderveer's mill was pre-Revolutionary.

PLATE 195

SCHENCK HOUSE

Early part of 1700. Taken down in 1930 and partly rebuilt inside the Brooklyn Museum.

Bohn Negative.

VANDERVEER HOUSE, FLATBUSH, L. I.

Built 1787. No longer standing in 1911.

PLATE 196

Bohn Negative.

ELSIE GARRETSEN HOUSE,
FLATBUSH AVENUE NEAR FENIMORE STREET, BROOKLYN
Built about 1781.

PLATE 197

AMORY-TICKNOR HOUSE, BOSTON

Built about 1803. Altered later. Detail looking through front door from vestibule.

PLATE 198

EZEKIEL HERSEY DERBY HOUSE, 204–6 ESSEX STREET, SALEM

*1799—Arches and doorways by Bulfinch. Later residence of Benjamin W. Crowninshield
and residence of Richard Rogers, 1817. Bought of William Maynes, 1874,
and altered to Maynes Block, 1908.*

PLATE 199

CHAPIN TAVERN, CHICOPEE, MASS.

Tap room chamber.

Plate 200

Courtesy of the Society for the Preservation of New England Antiquities.

CHAPIN TAVERN, CHICOPEE, MASS.

Northwest chamber fireplace.

Courtesy of the Society for the Preservation of New England Antiquities.

CHAPIN TAVERN, CHICOPEE, MASS.

Tap room fireplace.

PLATE 201

Courtesy of the Society for the Preservation of New England Antiquities.

CHAPIN TAVERN, CHICOPEE, MASS.

PLATE 202

GEORGE JAFFREY HOUSE, PORTSMOUTH, N. H.

*Showing window reveals and woodwork in original position. Built about 1730.
Demolished 1920.*

PLATE 203

EZEKIEL HERSEY DERBY HOUSE, 204–6 ESSEX STREET, SALEM

By Bulfinch, 1799.

PLATE 204

MANSION HOUSE, CHARLESTON, S. C.
Built circa 1765. Wall panel, drawing room, second floor.

MANSION HOUSE, CHARLESTON, S. C.
Built circa 1765. Panelled end of back room, second floor.

PLATE 205

Courtesy of Charles W. Stoughton, Esq.

ROGER MORRIS HOUSE (JUMEL MANSION), NEW YORK CITY

*Built 1765. Interior view taken looking through into octagonal drawing room in which
Washington held a council of war. This photograph taken in 1886 when the house was
occupied by a Mr. Chase, collaterally of the original family. This shows the family
furniture and the original wallpaper as in occupation. The house is now a museum.*

PLATE 206

ROGER MORRIS HOUSE (JUMEL MANSION), NEW YORK CITY
Built 1765. This photograph was taken in 1886. The house is now a museum.

ROGER MORRIS HOUSE (JUMEL MANSION), NEW YORK CITY
*Built 1765. Interior view taken from extreme front room looking through to the back.
This photograph was taken in 1886 when the house was occupied by a Mr. Chase,
collaterally of the original family. This shows the family furniture and
the original wallpaper as in occupation. The house is now a museum.*

Plate 207

JOSEPH BARRELL HOUSE, CHARLESTOWN (LATER SOMERVILLE), MASS.

Niche showing interior detail. Built 1792. Taken down 1898.

PLATE 208

PEREZ MORTON HOUSE, ROXBURY, MASS.

Ceiling in stair cage.

AMORY-TICKNOR HOUSE, BOSTON

Built about 1803. Interior detail of wall niche and pilasters.

PLATE 209

MANSION HOUSE, CHARLESTON, S. C.

Built circa 1767. Drawing room mantel.

PLATE 210

PEREZ MORTON HOUSE, ROXBURY, MASS.

Hall with coved ceiling.

PLATE 211

PANELLING IN HEWLETT HOUSE, WOODBURY, L. I.

PLATE 212

OLD HOUSE OF AN EARLY PERIOD IN WASHINGTON STREET, PORTSMOUTH, N. H.

Demolished in 1927. Panelled end of first floor room.

PLATE 213

COMBS HOUSE, NEWBURYPORT

Mantel.

George E. Noyes Negative.

PLATE 214

HALL AT 71 STATE STREET, NEWBURYPORT

Purchased by the Society for the Preservation of New England Antiquities.

PLATE 215

STAIRCASE

Without balusters from pre-Revolutionary house at Kittery Point.
Taken down 1926.

GEORGE JAFFREY HOUSE, PORTSMOUTH, N. H.

Detail of front entrance. Built about 1730. Demolished 1920.

Plate 216

George E. Noyes Negative.

Early Type of Stair, Newburyport

Unknown house, now destroyed.

PLATE 217

OLD HOUSE OF AN EARLY PERIOD IN WASHINGTON STREET, PORTSMOUTH, N. H.
Demolished in 1927. Stairway on ground floor.

PLATE 218

CABOT-LEE-KILHAM HOUSE, 115 CABOT STREET, BEVERLY, MASS.

Stairway. Built 1773. Lately destroyed to make way for a gasoline station.

PLATE 219

CALEB MILLS HOUSE, MEDFORD, MASS.

Newel and four balustrades. Destroyed in 1919.

PLATE 220

Courtesy of the Essex Institute.

TIMOTHY ORNE HOUSE, 266 ESSEX STREET, SALEM

Stairway. Later residence of Benjamin Hodges. Taken down before 1913.
Possibly in some other house.

PLATE 221

FRONT STAIRS, CHAPIN TAVERN, CHICOPEE, MASS.

Plate 222

AMORY-TICKNOR HOUSE, BOSTON

Built about 1803. Staircase. Altered later.

PLATE 223

FIRST BAPTIST CHURCH IN THE U. S., NEWPORT, R. I.

*Showing pews in position. Photograph presented by Charles F. McKim to
W. D. Howells in 1875.*

Plate 224

GEORGE JAFFREY HOUSE, PORTSMOUTH, N. H.

*Built about 1739. Demolished 1920. Showing corner cupboard before removal
to Boston Art Museum.*

PLATE 225

Nash Negative.

CUPBOARD, HUNT MANSION, HUNTS POINT, N. Y.

Plate 226

CUPBOARD AND DETAILS, HEWLETT HOUSE, WOODBURY, L. I.

Photograph of woodwork in original position before removal to Metropolitan Museum of Art.

PLATE 227

AMASA DAVIS HOUSE, WASHINGTON STREET, BOSTON, MASS.

Plate 228

DUDLEY WOODBRIDGE HOUSE, 48 BRIDGE STREET, SALEM

*Mantel, first floor. Built about 1786. As McIntire's original plan for this house exists,
Dr. Fiske Kimball regards this mantelpiece as by McIntire himself.*

PLATE 229

Courtesy of the Essex Institute.

DUDLEY WOODBRIDGE HOUSE, 48 BRIDGE STREET, SALEM

Mantel, first floor. Built about 1786. As McIntire's original plan for this house exists,
Dr. Fiske Kimball regards this mantelpiece as by McIntire himself.

PLATE 230

AMORY-TICKNOR HOUSE, BOSTON

Built about 1803. Interior detail of cornice and pilaster.

PLATE 231

MANTELPIECE, RAPALJI HOUSE, 349 NEW LOTS ROAD, BROOKLYN

Now destroyed.

Plate 232

Fireplace, Hunt Mansion, Hunts Point, N. Y.

Courtesy of the Essex Institute.

MANTEL, EZEKIEL HERSEY DERBY HOUSE, 286 (140 OLD NUMBER), LAFAYETTE STREET, SALEM
Before 1802. Later Lafayette House Taken down before 1890. Mantel by Samuel McIntire.

PLATE 234

WOOD MANTEL, EZEKIEL HERSEY DERBY HOUSE, 204–6 ESSEX STREET, SALEM

PLATE 235

PANELLING, EZEKIEL HERSEY DERBY HOUSE, 204–6 ESSEX STREET, SALEM

PLATE 236

PUTNAM-HANSON HOUSE, 94 BOSTON STREET, SALEM

Woodwork by McIntire. Photo shows original wallpaper.

Plate 237

Mantel from Jonathan Mansfield House, Norman Street, Salem

Removed to Albert Goodhue House, 47 Warren Street, Salem.

Plate 238

Urns by Samuel McIntire

From South Church steeple. Now in Essex Institute.

PLATE 239

JOSEPH MANIGAULT GATE LODGE, CHARLESTON, S. C.

Gabriel Manigault, Architect. Now altered and used as a filling station. Built about 1790.

PLATE 240

OLD "GUN HOUSE" ARSENAL, PORTSMOUTH, N. H.

Built 1808. Demolition date unknown.

POWDER HOUSE, PORTSMOUTH, N. H.

Built 1811. Destruction date unknown.

PLATE 241

PUTNAM-HANSON HOUSE, 94 BOSTON STREET, SALEM
Photo shows original wallpaper.

PLATE 242

GEORGE JAFFREY HOUSE, PORTSMOUTH, N. H.

Close up of corner, showing two types of clapboarding, the narrow ones on the right showing the ship-lapped joints. Built about 1730. Demolished 1920.

PLATE 243

Courtesy of the Society for the Preservation of New England Antiquities.

BARN ORIGINALLY ON ELIAS HASKETT DERBY FARM

Judged to be by McIntire, since he did all of this owner's work. Now removed and re-erected elsewhere. Built between 1775 and 1800.

PLATE 244

OLD BLOCKHOUSE, FORT MCCLARY, KITTERY POINT, MAINE

Shown before present restoration but without drawbridge or ladder which originally let down by chains from the doorway, and of which parts of the hinges still show at foot of door trim.

INDEX

OF BUILDINGS, LOCATIONS, ARCHITECTS AND DESIGNERS

The Numbers Refer to the Plates.

Dover Books on Art

PINE FURNITURE OF EARLY NEW ENGLAND, R. H. Kettell. Over 400 illustrations, over 50 working drawings of early New England chairs, benches, beds, cupboards, mirrors, shelves, tables, other furniture esteemed for simple beauty and character. "Rich store of illustrations . . . emphasizes the individuality and varied design," ANTIQUES. 413 illustrations, 55 working drawings. 475pp. 8 x 10¾. T145 Clothbound $10.00

BASIC BOOKBINDING, A. W. Lewis. Enables both beginners and experts to rebind old books or bind paperbacks in hard covers. Treats materials, tools; gives step-by-step instruction in how to collate a book, sew it, back it, make boards, etc. 261 illus. Appendices. 155pp. 5⅜ x 8. T169 Paperbound $1.45

DESIGN MOTIFS OF ANCIENT MEXICO, J. Enciso. Nearly 90% of these 766 superb designs from Aztec, Olmec, Totonac, Maya, and Toltec origins are unobtainable elsewhere. Contains plumed serpents, wind gods, animals, demons, dancers, monsters, etc. Excellent applied design source. Originally $17.50. 766 illustrations, thousands of motifs. 192pp. 6⅛ x 9¼. T84 Paperbound $1.85

A DIDEROT PICTORIAL ENCYCLOPEDIA OF TRADES AND INDUSTRY. Manufacturing and the Technical Arts in Plates Selected from "L'Encyclopédie ou Dictionnaire Raisonné des Sciences, des Arts, et des Métiers," of Denis Diderot, edited with text by C. Gillispie. Over 2000 illustrations on 485 full-page plates. Magnificent 18th-century engravings of men, women, and children working at such trades as milling flour, cheesemaking, charcoal burning, mining, silverplating, shoeing horses, making fine glass, printing, hundreds more, showing details of machinery, different steps in sequence, etc. A remarkable art work, but also the largest collection of working figures in print, copyright-free, for art directors, designers, etc. Two vols. 920pp. 9 x 12. Heavy library cloth. T421 Two volume set $18.50

SILK SCREEN TECHNIQUES, J. Biegeleisen, M. Cohn. A practical step-by-step home course in one of the most versatile, least expensive graphic arts processes. How to build an inexpensive silk screen, prepare stencils, print, achieve special textures, use color, etc. Every step explained, diagrammed. 149 illustrations, 201pp. 6⅛ x 9¼. T433 Paperbound $1.55

STICKS AND STONES, Lewis Mumford. An examination of forces influencing American architecture: the medieval tradition in early New England, the classical influence in Jefferson's time, the Brown Decades, the imperial facade, the machine age, etc. "A truly remarkable book," SAT. REV. OF LITERATURE. 2nd revised edition. 21 illus. xvii + 240pp. 5⅜ x 8. T202 Paperbound $1.65

THE AUTOBIOGRAPHY OF AN IDEA, Louis Sullivan. The architect whom Frank Lloyd Wright called "the master," records the development of the theories that revolutionized America's skyline. 34 full-page plates of Sullivan's finest work. New introduction by R. M. Line. xiv + 335pp. 5⅜ x 8. T281 Paperbound $2.00

ART ANATOMY, Dr. William Rimmer. One of the few books on art anatomy that are themselves works of art, this is a faithful reproduction (rearranged for handy use) of the extremely rare masterpiece of the famous 19th century anatomist, sculptor, and art teacher. Beautiful, clear line drawings show every part of the body—bony structure, muscles, features, etc. Unusual are the sections on falling bodies, foreshortenings, muscles in tension, grotesque personalities, and Rimmer's remarkable interpretation of emotions and personalities as expressed by facial features. It will supplement every other book on art anatomy you are likely to have. Reproduced clearer than the lithographic original (which sells for $500 on up on the rare book market.) Over 1,200 illustrations. xᵢii + 153pp. 7¾ x 10¾.

T908 Paperbound $2.00

THE CRAFTSMAN'S HANDBOOK, Cennino Cennini. The finest English translation of IL LIBRO DELL' ARTE, the 15th century introduction to art technique that is both a mirror of Quatrocento life and a source of many useful but nearly forgotten facets of the painter's art. 4 illustrations. xxvii + 142pp. D. V. Thompson, translator. 5⅜ x 8. T54 Paperbound $1.50

THE BROWN DECADES, Lewis Mumford. A picture of the "buried renaissance" of the post-Civil War period, and the founding of modern architecture (Sullivan, Richardson, Root, Roebling), landscape development (Marsh, Olmstead, Eliot), and the graphic arts (Homer, Eakins, Ryder). 2nd revised, enlarged edition. Bibliography. 12 illustrations. xiv + 266 pp. 5⅜ x 8.

T200 Paperbound $1.75

THE STYLES OF ORNAMENT, A. Speltz. The largest collection of line ornament in print, with 3750 numbered illustrations arranged chronologically from Egypt, Assyria, Greeks, Romans, Etruscans, through Medieval, Renaissance, 18th century, and Victorian. No permissions, no fees needed to use or reproduce illustrations. 400 plates with 3750 illustrations. Bibliography. Index. 640pp. 6 x 9. T577 Paperbound $2.50

THE ART OF ETCHING, E. S. Lumsden. Every step of the etching process from essential materials to completed proof is carefully and clearly explained, with 24 annotated plates exemplifying every technique and approach discussed. The book also features a rich survey of the art, with 105 annotated plates by masters. Invaluable for beginner to advanced etcher. 374pp. 5⅜ x 8. T49 Paperbound $2.50

OF THE JUST SHAPING OF LETTERS, Albrecht Dürer. This remarkable volume reveals Albrecht Dürer's rules for the geometric construction of Roman capitals and the formation of Gothic lower case and capital letters, complete with construction diagrams and directions. Of considerable practical interest to the contemporary illustrator, artist, and designer. Translated from the Latin text of the edition of 1535 by R. T. Nichol. Numerous letterform designs, construction diagrams, illustrations. iv + 43pp. 7⅞ x 10¾. T1306 Paperbound $1.25

PRINCIPLES OF ART HISTORY, H. Wölfflin. This remarkably instructive work demonstrates the tremendous change in artistic conception from the 14th to the 18th centuries, by analyzing 164 works by Botticelli, Dürer, Hobbema, Holbein, Hals, Titian, Rembrandt, Vermeer, etc., and pointing out exactly what is meant by "baroque," "classic," "primitive," "picturesque," and other basic terms of art history and criticism. "A remarkable lesson in the art of seeing," SAT. REV. OF LITERATURE. Translated from the 7th German edition. 150 illus. 254pp. 6⅛ x 9¼.   T276 Paperbound $2.00

FOUNDATIONS OF MODERN ART, A. Ozenfant. Stimulating discussion of human creativity from paleolithic cave painting to modern painting, architecture, decorative arts. Fully illustrated with works of Gris, Lipchitz, Léger, Picasso, primitive, modern artifacts, architecture, industrial art, much more. 226 illustrations. 368pp. 6⅛ x 9¼.   T215 Paperbound $2.00

METALWORK AND ENAMELLING, H. Maryon. Probably the best book ever written on the subject. Tells everything necessary for the home manufacture of jewelry, rings, ear pendants, bowls, etc. Covers materials, tools, soldering, filigree, setting stones, raising patterns, repoussé work, damascening, niello, cloisonné, polishing, assaying, casting, and dozens of other techniques. The best substitute for apprenticeship to a master metalworker. 363 photos and figures. 374pp. 5½ x 8½.
                                    T183 Clothbound $8.50

SHAKER FURNITURE, E. D. and *F. Andrews.* The most illuminating study of Shaker furniture ever written. Covers chronology, craftsmanship, houses, shops, etc. Includes over 200 photographs of chairs, tables, clocks, beds, benches, etc. "Mr. & Mrs. Andrews know all there is to know about Shaker furniture," Mark Van Doren, NATION. 48 full-page plates. 192pp. 7⅞ x 10¾.   T679 Paperbound $2.00

LETTERING AND ALPHABETS, J. A. Cavanagh. An unabridged reissue of "Lettering," containing the full discussion, analysis, illustration of 89 basic hand lettering styles based on Caslon, Bodoni, Gothic, many other types. Hundreds of technical hints on construction, strokes, pens, brushes, etc. 89 alphabets, 72 lettered specimens, which may be reproduced permission-free. 121pp. 9¾ x 8.   T53 Paperbound $1.35

THE HUMAN FIGURE IN MOTION, Eadweard Muybridge. The largest collection in print of Muybridge's famous high-speed action photos. 4789 photographs in more than 500 action-strip-sequences (at shutter speeds up to 1/6000th of a second) illustrate men, women, children—mostly undraped—performing such actions as walking, running, getting up, lying down, carrying objects, throwing, etc. "An unparalleled dictionary of action for all artists," AMERICAN ARTIST. 390 full-page plates, with 4789 photographs. Heavy glossy stock, reinforced binding with headbands. 7⅞ x 10¾.   T204 Clothbound $10.00

Dover Books on Art

LANDSCAPE GARDENING IN JAPAN, Josiah Conder. A detailed picture of Japanese gardening techniques and ideas, the artistic principles incorporated in the Japanese garden, and the religious and ethical concepts at the heart of those principles. Preface. 92 illustrations, plus all 40 full-page plates from the Supplement. Index. xv + 299pp. 8⅜ x 11¼.

T1216 Paperbound $2.75

DESIGN AND FIGURE CARVING, E. J. Tangerman. "Anyone who can peel a potato can carve," states the author, and in this unusual book he shows you how, covering every stage in detail from very simple exercises working up to museum-quality pieces. Terrific aid for hobbyists, arts and crafts counselors, teachers, those who wish to make reproductions for the commercial market. Appendix: How to Enlarge a Design. Brief bibliography. Index. 1298 figures. x + 289pp. 5⅜ x 8½.

T1209 Paperbound $1.85

THE STANDARD BOOK OF QUILT MAKING AND COLLECTING, M. Ickis. Even if you are a beginner, you will soon find yourself quilting like an expert, by following these clearly drawn patterns, photographs, and step-by-step instructions. Learn how to plan the quilt, to select the pattern to harmonize with the design and color of the room, to choose materials. Over 40 full-size patterns. Index. 483 illustrations. One color plate. xi + 276pp. 6¾ x 9½.

T582 Paperbound $2.00

LOST EXAMPLES OF COLONIAL ARCHITECTURE, J. M. Howells. This book offers a unique guided tour through America's architectural past, all of which is either no longer in existence or so changed that its original beauty has been destroyed. More than 275 clear photos of old churches, dwelling houses, public buildings, business structures, etc. 245 plates, containing 281 photos and 9 drawings, floorplans, etc. New Index. xvii + 248pp. 7⅞ x 10¾.

T1143 Paperbound $2.75

A HISTORY OF COSTUME, Carl Köhler. The most reliable and authentic account of the development of dress from ancient times through the 19th century. Based on actual pieces of clothing that have survived, using paintings, statues and other reproductions only where originals no longer exist. Hundreds of illustrations, including detailed patterns for many articles. Highly useful for theatre and movie directors, fashion designers, illustrators, teachers. Edited and augmented by Emma von Sichart. Translated by Alexander K. Dallas. 594 illustrations. 464pp. 5⅛ x 7⅛.

T1030 Paperbound $2.75

Dover publishes books on commercial art, art history, crafts, design, art classics; also books on music, literature, science, mathematics, puzzles and entertainments, chess, engineering, biology, philosophy, psychology, languages, history, and other fields. For free circulars write to Dept. DA, Dover Publications, Inc., 180 Varick St., New York, N.Y. 10014.